For the Girl Inside and Ones Like Her

E.G.

I know that someday I will be in a better place than today,

just as I am in a better place now than before.

(For the ways we want to live and don't.)

Trigger Warning:

This book discusses self-harm, disordered eating, and mental illness.

For the Girl Inside and Ones Like Her is a collection of thoughts from the past two years of my life, from seventeen to nineteen.

We grew up here.

We loved hard here.

We are honest here.

I learned that there are so many bright, lovely things to stay alive for, but I remember how hard it used to be to find them.

I wrote this for the girl inside me, who I haven't always treated as she deserved, and who I hope to continue to learn to love better until the day I die.

I wrote this for the ones like her.

To the ones who aren't quite home, but they want to be.

To the ones who have battled the darkest days of their lives and are on the journey upwards.

To the ones who feel like they have not found their place, their purpose yet,

You are not alone.

You are never alone

Wishing Well:

11/11/19

There is a hollow and crossroads steeping inside me.

I feel quiet.

(You feel too good to be true.)

Will you,

        my Love,

                sing me to sleep?

Crying would be easier than writing

but tears disappear and poems do not always.

Let us shape something on our inside shelves.

Let us mold something beautiful to sell.

re Dead Ends Meet:

Safety is an insecure word.

He is a wonderful one who does not believe it.

Cut through the cul de sac.

I rest at the bottom of

we'll see.

Are emotions inundating our veins to be battled or sighed?

A field of waving science is either the end to possible or

beginning to impossible.

Writing ends and begins me.

He is, singularly, another answer;

The past is in the past.

Darling, Darling, Dear,

do not cry for being damaged.

Every leaving was a lesson,

every lesson leaves you with a new skill.

Yes, like how to cry at a measly uphill word.

Yes, like how to stay still when they are raging on
unsettled; your discomfort will wait for a quieter
time.
Yes, like how to leave the night in transparent tears,
he mustn't know.

After coffee cake and goodnight kisses,
a warm blanket, soft hand,
we will leave trauma by the banked fire.
We will be a calm sea again.

Every Song Lyric was Written by Somebody (I Aspire to be Somebody):

Featured in Issue I of The Latte Edit Autumn 2020, Get Lost

You know I hate to be Loved for the way I write

(which, of course, makes being a writer an irony)

more because

to be shallow

I think I write better than I look

or to be deep

I write better than I live

and I am the overdone type of girl

who would rather be Loved where I am

if I am to be Loved

(she still carries the fear you gave her of assumption)

for the way I sit next to you

or the kindness that jumps from my innocent hands into

other innocent hands and back

than for the cursive notions

that trickle sometimes

sometimes pour

through the channels first Death drove deep

into the fresh fields that are fresh no longer

to be graphic

like dripping ink

to be mild

like the ditches rain races green dragonflies in

You know I long to be held for the ways I find to speak.

Violin:

My overeager ear

reaches for

something more

than I am

and may ever be.

I say,

> *No,*

> > *This is today.*

> > > *This is where we are*

> > > > *now.*

But my overeager ear

will not listen.

Why, God, do I always want more?

Is it a lack of taming my weakness,

or is it a purposeful displacement?

> *Where does Restlessness like mine belong?*

I am so sad.

I don't know how to be less or more.

I want to be less and more.

I am not a child.

I am not grown.

It has been four long and strange years since t

Still I wonder who I am.

/

I am so sad

that I will hold whatever children I am blessed with

in arms and scars I cannot erase.

How am I going to answer their white questions?

I don't want them to learn their first sadness

from touching me.

Reversed:

We have tried too hard to make the wounded feel loved

and in turn have made the whole feel left out and imperfect

in their perfection.

Ugliness is beauty.

Beauty is unwanted.

My Mother is Korean-American:

My Mother is Korean-American.

Korean, she is an American.

Where she grew up the only people of her color were:

Her, her two brothers, and one other adoptee.

Do you smell rice?

Was the greeting she met with.

Little tomboy,

but girls aren't supposed to play sports.

Friendship and betrayal.

Middle schooler grinding baby powder into golden arms

and knees.

Sunscreen, cover up.

Skin, please don't get darker.

Forcing eyes wide open, anything to look more like them.

Why can I not be one of them?

I love West Virginia and her mountains

but her people of the 70's and 80's could be so cruel.

She was Alone half the time 'til she met my father,

then Alone most of the time.

My parents are an edifice of an example that two halves do
not always equate to whole.

Looking at this I reached the threshold of the recent
obsession with heritage.

It feels powerful to take what bruised our parents and tell it,

　　　No.

Some of these adopted, immigrated shadows did not have
that option.

Some of them spoke

and were heard only as an accent,

seen only as a pair of slanted eyes

enough to tell them foreigners did not understand their

어머니, *madre, Mutter*

tongue

nor care to.

　　　No, you are the foreigner. You cannot argue that.

My Mother is Korean-American.

Her surroundings have never asked her to stand tall beside

the jet black, the crimson, the jade, the cobalt, the opal.

She grew up believing that she should be anything, anyone

else.

Would not you too, want to burn down the country you

were born in

if you were not allowed to forget

you smelled like 김치,

like kimchi,

whether or not you had ever tasted it?

My daughters and sons will know,

      Love is the answer to someone different than you.

Regardless how much

나는 혼합 문화를 좋아한다,

I Love my mixed culture,

I can not make up for what was ingrained in her childhood.

Irreparable damage is not fixed by tiny words like this.

Mother, see yourself.

You are everything too grand to call beautiful,

too strong to be strength,

and all the gold in me.

Stop Sign:

There's something about the soft light

and being on my way to you

that turns my heart in a different way than it has been.

You make me a happier person.

Here We Fall:

Following drying dishes and skim milk,

I like to take the things I do not like,

> *(i.e., sticky summers, ice cubes, gravel)*

and the things I am unable to comprehend,

> *(i.e., death, dreams, how she could have left)*

and knit them into strolling chapters

that move like chess pieces across a checkered plain

that I may pretend to understand what I do not.

Because if you write about a sweetheart's freckles, or curves,

or elbows

you sound in Love,

and if you sing about

how being abandoned is a vacant house with a crumbling

'tenant wanted' sign in front

someone will harmonize,

and if you say,

> *We are universes.*

you hand out an addictive, unearned special.

You get to feel like a good person

when people praise you for it.

And if you scribble out collections of arid poetry titled
romantically

     *(i.e., When Love Begins, For the Girl Inside and
Ones Like Her)*
your close family circle and maybe a couple friends will call
you a writer, an artist,
and if you hear something enough times,

     *(i.e., you are the best I have ever found, you are next
best to the last one)*
somewhere, your vain, ticking cognition will begin to
believe it
and you will be too shy early on
and later, too convinced
to correct them.

Words That Make a Drooping Poem (The Poet Isn't Home):

Sadness is a cobweb.

You brush it off,

then brush it off,

then brush it off.

There are more important things than what's going on in

your little mind.

You brush it off,

then brush it off,

then brush it off.

It clings.

He brushes it off for me when my arms are tired

yet phantom fingers hold mine.

I'm fine

but sadness is a cobweb

and sadness stays.

/

I carry loneliness or loneliness drags me.

Either way, we are partners for life.

It isn't your fault;

the emptiness in wanting and waiting.

/

How can you tell you're good at something?

You see the unseen before it arrives.

Here and There:

Creation finds and loses me in such a hot and cold

whirlwind

the wind struggles to reach me.

I am here and then there

then there and there and there.

A nest?

I think there is no such comfortable thing.

Inside out is my world when time does not allow Art and I

to connect over tea and watercolor.

I have not been a poet for a year.

A musician, and artist, still,

Not a poet.

When Love Begins

was where the words of the teenage season must have ended,

for I have not found them since the pages were printed for

others' eyes.

Come back to me,

make me yours again.

I miss you.

Come back to me.

Honey:

All I need is one who knows how to love me.

Here.

Now.

More:

You've always wanted the ones who grew past darknesses.

Why are you not one of them?

Girl Inside, be better.

You are not only this,

you are not only writer,

only the haunting, hurt places.

Everyone knows those are the ones that stand out

so decorate another part of your body

with ink or color or happiness.

Show yourself there's more in this world than what was.

Exploration:

I'm on a trip to discover a new world for myself,

too many have landed on the old one

and I have grown too.

I'm trying,

I'm trying,

I'm trying

to look at myself

and

see.

It's hard.

I haven't been into self-discovery since I was excited to find

out what thumped in my chest.

Cynical.

Does writing remember me?

It's hard to hold on to art that is ready to grow up

without you.

Between myself and my other self

I am a sliver of time

waiting to be found.

Find me.

In the Clouds:

You are my first thought and my sweetest one.

I love the ways we love each other.

Slow or in the ordinary and when we have been missing.

When I Walk:

The age of fourteen has been on my mind.

It was such a young girl there,

it was such a dark girl there.

Yet sometimes I think she knew who she was better than I

do now,

at eighteen.

Four dragging years here

and no better direction.

I'm sorry,

it is so much better here.

The walk tires me

though and

I just want to know

where it will end.

/

Once, I was fourteen going on eternity.

I looked for heaven in hell.

Draped in shivers and unnatural sadness,

> *Dark haired honey.*

> *Oh, for white hallways.*

A guitar playing nurse.

Eat something, for once.

I thought I was invisible.

That, at least, has lasted.

It still surprises me when someone knows my name.

Like if you don't know what I've been how do you know
what to call me,

like you don't expect a stranger to wave at you,

like you don't want your reflection to talk back.

Let me look.

Don't look at me.

Just write it like you mean it.

Who will find you here?

You're talking about fourteen,

not today, right?

Eighteen is what it should be and what it wants to be
except here.

Everywhere but here.

You are pulling your own disguising curtain aside.

Her Perspective:

He puts his hands on me

and the voice inside screams

This!

This is not Love!

But I know

I will wake up next to him tomorrow

and I will tell myself it is

because after twenty five years,

it is still easier than saying goodbye.

Things We Lived For:

My generation,

walks and long talks and coffee shops.

Things we stayed alive for

when all we wanted was not to.

/

I hurt from a place inside my chest

where my mother never saw me,

where I never trusted my father.

How can you look at your child's scars of self-harm and still

say you have to be the one in control?

I suppose she, too, hurts in a place unseen.

/

I miss the people who used to love me.

Not Really a Dream:

(After happiness is a butterfly by Lana del Ray)

I've been up with the butterflies

waiting for you to love me.

I'm in love

and I'm lonely

and nothing I ask finds an answer I can hear

and restlessness, restlessness, restless

keeps building her home in me.

The girl inside.

The girl inside.

The girl inside

is not me.

/

I have this sick feeling

like I'm standing on the edge of a world

wishing it would end

but it keeps spinning and spinning and

I remember

when I walked the crimson fields

and told everyone that they didn't

love me.

And told myself

that

I deserved it.

And my mother,

she was nowhere

because I made her be nowhere.

And my sister,

she was everywhere in the wrong way

because I made her be in the wrong.

And I was disappearing and I was sick and I loved it

because I was hollow and hollow was salvation,

but not really.

I was dying.

It's hard to think that and harder to say it.

I know I'm on the edge now and not inside the past

but

I remember.

I'm supposed to be getting ready for my normal job and

my normal life

but I'm standing in the bathroom thinking,

I didn't have to be that girl

and I was

for so long

and I still miss her.

What's wrong with me that I miss a person like that

when I have everything now?

There's no answer.

But I remember.

/

We will have better days

but I wonder

if the girl inside knows that too.

I'm trying to tell her.

Algorithm:

Shouldn't I have been noticed by now?

Shouldn't I have found the indie writers' club that warms

me and brings me inside?

I still walk alone.

> (I can't shake my mother off my shadow.)

I promised myself I would write all the things that scared me

but

> I am afraid she's listening outside the door.

In the Process of Saying Goodbye:

I'd die to be loved.

I don't mean to say I do not feel loved

only that

I am lonely.

Don't take it as an accusation

I can't help it, I have tried.

Believe me.

Where is belonging and where is fullness?

I have neither and I cry for both to come quickly.

They never hear.

My childhood won't release me.

God, I try to run away.

> *I don't want to be your daughter anymore*, I
>
> said.

I found an escape plan and it let me down.

You think I'm hard on myself now

you should have seen me then.

Do I reach for a dream or for a future?

Rain:

This cloud formed from nothing.

Yesterday I was happy,

inspired even.

Tonight I fall in grey.

Again!

Always again!

Maybe I want to be

somebody

too badly to be more than myself.

If I Were Speaking to My Mother I Would Say: Pt I

I eat after a fight and it surprises me.

This is not what used to be;

A two day emptiness after

you tell me I am not doing enough.

>   *I am doing everything my soul knows,* I try.

But all that comes out-

>   *I'm trying.*

And you say,

>   *Try harder,*

 and walk into a house I cannot enter.

I tread the yard barefoot.

You say,

>   *You're missing your shoes.*

>   *The Internet is dangerous.*

I say,

>   *That does not make us want to be alone.*

Good example, bad example.

Who you are is not your own.

Stay where we don't want you.

It's wrong of you to go.

Freedom is right here if you will only look like us

and talk like us

and think like us.

There is nothing wrong here.

If I Were Speaking to My Mother I Would Say: Pt II

I loved you when you didn't know it and still you could

throw it away.

There's smallness in wanting.

It was growing to find I was needed.

Just as I am.

If there's anywhere to go I want to be on my way there.

I need to leave home but I want a place to stay.

I want a mother who knows my name

without me asking her to read and remember it every time

we say hello.

Love cannot stop where our similarities do

or no one is ever in love and no one ever knows what

warmth feels like.

I hug you and you say you're hugging back

but your arms stay at your side,

and I know that in your mind they are wrapped around me

but in my reality you are still stone cold.

Seasons change and I grow bigger in the mind and in the

center of courage.

I don't know where you are.

The garden we planted grows far beneath my skin.

I shrivel and bloom through my eyes.

No one looks at me the way I look at them.

I think I love you and I think you love me too.

I think we both know that we have so many things to
unfold between us

but neither of us knows where the end is.

We're afraid to keep walking when we can't see past the
edge.

I know you're my mother and you know I'm your daughter.

We don't feel like flesh and blood anymore.

Because I like tattoos and being a someone else,

because you like natural, what will people think, and long
words,

we think that that's all there is to both of us.

I know there's a way around this but I think it will take a
long time away from here to find it.

I have to have my own home before I'm okay in yours again.

You used to know me.

I used to think I knew you.

You still won't tell me about your first kiss and I wonder
what happened

that you will not tell your daughter about it.

Butterflies rain the ground purple.

Stars twinkle but they know that there is no resolving this
tonight.

Stop asking me to tell you who I am.

Stop asking me to be you.

Daughters don't have to be their mothers to be good
enough.

I'm in my own love and season.

You can't come in.

Today Says:

You thought you were grown up.

    Come back to Childhood.

        She misses your sadness.

            She misses your defeated walk.

I knew I hadn't outrun half the secrets haunting me,

but midconversation

they struck.

It's because of my mother I'm a people pleaser.

It was never enough for her.

It's because of my father I don't lead.

Quiet, quiet, and never ever confront.

You can't stand up to a man that loud when you have only

another's voice.

Let me be.

Let me be.

Let me be.

You Will not Find Anything but Restlessness Here:

If you find who you think you are

stay there.

Drop an anchor,

build a house

bury yourself on the spot.

Whatever it takes to stay.

I did not do that when I should have.

Regret chews the insides of my cheeks.

I bleed.

I spit and

this

small

frightened

newborn

shivering

misunderstood

shadowy

pink

book drops to the cement.

Don't use an adjective to make yourself smaller.

You've wasted enough time on that.

TAKE UP THE SPACE.

Insides Still Rot After Every Rain:

Every time I think I've finally left insecurity in the dark
behind me
she taps me on the shoulder and sends her shivers down my
spine.
My parents call from younger years,

> *We expected you to apologize.*

> *Now you assume*
> *everyone else wants you to apologize.*
> *It doesn't mean you're good at owning up.*
> *It means you take the fall whether it's yours to take or*

not.

> *You get your pride from your father and*
> *you didn't cut enough to cut him out.*
> *Keep going.*

I swear if there's ever going to be a place where small things
are not tied to other small things
that are tied to other small things that are tied to big things
that are tied to big fights
I will find my way there.

I hate that nothing I see is standing unconnected and it

makes me hate myself.

I hate that everything reminds me of when I would have cut

or skipped a meal

for the same thing two years ago.

Sometimes I hate that I don't still punish myself in those

ways

because deep down,

I still believe I deserve it.

Deeper still than that, I know it's all a lie.

I get afraid that Love will get afraid of me.

Therapy would help I think,

but help costs money and

the way I write isn't popular enough to pay for that.

House Guests:

My insecurities come out to play when I have banned them
to the back room.

They aren't supposed to show themselves when company is
over.

They aren't supposed to speak unless spoken to.

/

I'm afraid I am never honest.

I can't see past what has been.

/

Dissociation is my mask whenever I get close to breaking
through the walls

that make me feel so far away and small.

It's a bad habit from my leaving stage;

When it was simpler to run and to pretend nothing was real.

Scars and skipped meals and fathers and fights.

None of them mattered if I told myself I wasn't really there,

that I would not be there next year or in ten years,

I would never have children who ask what's wrong with my
skin.

Can Heaven tell me how to undo that?

/

I'm better

but

I still carry Depression's Isolation.

God, the isolation.

I still carry Anxiety's dark fear.

I still carry my mother's and father's childhoods as well as

my own.

Unpacking can wait forever.

I still carry Ana in my ear.

She still whispers,

and that's on why I don't like to be alone.

My thoughts haven't been a safe place since I first hated

myself for not being someone else.

It grew and grew and grows,

that's why I ask him,

> *Do you really love me?*
>
> *Do you really care?*
>
> *I don't think you trust me.*

I don't think anyone truly understands me and it isn't fair.

Self-hatred is a giant towering over the world.

I don't know how to let those feelings go.

I am as sick of hearing them as he is

but I don't know

how

to stop

asking.

Now I Say Again:

In the back of a kitchen

in the afternoon

I spread myself thin

and ask,

>   *Why do you need so much of me?*

I shift and I transform,

and run and run and run,

but I always wake up in the same place at home.

I can't live here anymore.

Claustrophobia does not take me to material places.

Rather, in mind games and when I am told,

>   *No.*

He's a bad father.

I'm allowed to say that.

It can be black and white today.

Guilt holds me and squeezes me.

Even her strong hands aren't a safe place to stay now.

It's dangerous when my arms itch and I am hopeless.

Healing must begin.

I'm not wasting any more of my youth apologizing or

defending people who still put the blame on me.

I am a twisted girl but I want to work on it.

Now I say again,

Let me go.

Things That Have Been Said:

I don't want to be standing next to the casket of a thirteen year old.

I'm sorry you don't get the attention you think you need from this family.

I don't want you to leave.

Please try to eat.

You aren't being a good example.

You're showing signs of developing an eating disorder.

You're too pretty of a girl to be wearing long sleeves for the rest of your life.

Stop touching your arms. I know that look.

What is a healthy coping mechanism?

Eat something for once. Do you think I haven't noticed?

You're going to regret this for the rest of your life.

Do you hate yourself?

I don't want you passing out on us.

You're not fat. Just curvy. (I was eleven).

Has he ever been physically abusive though?

You have to stop hurting yourself. You're an adult now.

I'm here if you need me. I promise.

You can't let his actions control yours.

She's cut a lot.

Is it my fault?

These are just the consequences for your choices.

It's going to get better.

It could be worse.

Eden, you've mutilated yourself.

Youth Groups and Why We Leave Them:

When I was sadness,

I hid and I hid well

but I think about the people who left,

and the people who stayed longer,

and the people who stayed.

There were adults and friends among them,

and I haven't heard from almost all of them in months.

I know I'm not the girl who has the glow around her,

or the loudest voice in the room,

I just thought

someone would be asking,

or reaching out,

or caring after.

And they did and did,

but for how long?

I know I'm easy to forget

and I don't stand out much

but I love people

and people don't love me back the same.

There were adults and leaders.

Maybe it's bad to say,

but I think that's why young people leave churches.

If you don't want me for me

but for what I can do for you

I can't grow.

It's hard to believe that after knowing me and seeing my life

they would ask me again to

be a good example

and to give

when they did not pour into me the same way.

You should be serving more.

I needed you to be friends.

Love our daughters.

No, I'm still asking you to love

me.

11/24/20

I am so restless it makes me sick.

12/2/20

I wish my mother and I knew how to love each other.

I Used to Be:

I used to be a girl of the Church.

To the point that I hardly knew a bigger world.

I wanted more.

/

I used to be a girl undecided.

No clue who I was or how to get closer to her.

How I starved and cut whenever I went looking.

I was Godless and it was so dark.

When I saw the light,

I vowed never to go back to that place.

/

I used to be a girl of laughter.

I would say

I didn't know how to be sad.

I would be so angry with myself for not staying with the

serious things that rocked my world.

Pay attention.

I paid attention.

I think it broke me to look at the things that hurt.

I became frozen, staring at them until all I could see was the stains.

/

I used to be a girl alone.

Always, always, always, have I felt alone.

Like I'm inside out,

like I'm floating away from the crowd.

Still I feel it.

When I drive and at night it creeps in.

Solitude is a faithful friend.

/

I used to be a girl of music.

I played for ten years and then one day

I couldn't find it anymore.

I think it went to the same place my conscious did

when I kept telling it,

Not now.

/

My mother thinks I'm a bad person.

/

I used to be a girl with a family.

I have brothers and sisters but you wouldn't know it from

the way they look at me.

We talk about the days and friendship and TV shows.

We never talk about the week I went missing or

what it's like to survive our home.

They learned to stop asking,

What's wrong with your arms?

I think I'm the only one who sees the exit signs.

/

I used to be a girl with good character.

I didn't understand the teenage movies where all they care

about is drugs and sex.

I didn't know how to let four letter words slip out naturally.

I didn't know how to walk or talk or sit without feeling how

uncomfortable I was inside.

It took a long time for me to find a voice that wasn't anyone

else's.

/

I used to be a girl on a roof.

Watching the city go by while the preacher man finished up

below.

Wishing the church were a few stories higher so I could take

a breath as I fell.

I don't remember if there was ever a time

when I didn't run and run and run.

/

I used to be a girl of God.

I desperately want to find her again.

Though I know my actions don't always portray that

and I do things a good Christian girl shouldn't do.

I can't find God these days

but I know it's because I'm facing away from Him

and I'm not strong enough to turn the other way.

/

I used to be a girl of innocence and youth.

I called myself a teenage dreamer

and believed in so much good.

Moving Out:

When I leave my mother's home

I will never be a child again.

/

I don't want to be sad inside forever.

/

I just want to rest.

I just want to be understood.

/

She says I'm turning my back on God.

/

When the mirror talks to me she says I would be happy if I

were skinnier.

I've learned to tell her that I am only one of my problems.

12/11/20

Something is always going to be falling apart.

I have stopped wasting the time to notice.

Maybe that's why

I don't write much anymore.

When Hunger Bites my Hand:

It is night time.

I sit in my room as a silhouette

(not one of the slim, pretty ones)

and try to discover new ways to say I am thinking.

Pondering,

Musing over,

Coloring.

I am looking for a way to color an empty stomach

as something other than destructive.

> *It's just breakfast!*
>> *It's just lunch!*
>>> *It's just one day!*

I know it's in the past, and

Friend, I vowed not to go back there.

For real this time.

Still, I look for somewhere to spill my guts.

To him, to Him, to him.

To you, to words, to the gallery of old costumes in the closet

upstairs.

If I skip breakfast and lunch every other day

it keeps me ahead of the reverse cravings but on my way to
success.

/

A girl sits next to me during our break and I know she is
keeping herself together,

keeping herself small.

I want to cry and tell her,

No!

Don't shrink for me!

*I would never want you to be smaller than you want to be for
yourself!*

But life has been pulling at me.

I eat three bites of a sandwich and throw it away

and the girl does not know

that I am her friend

and that I love her as she is.

Pieces pt I:

My mother isn't the only one who doesn't recognize me.

I feel the blue seeping back into my bones;

                  Nothing sounds better than turning red.

I speak the way I watched my mother.

With twists and in the right light and at the right pace

so you don't know the secrets.

It isn't lying, it's just shadowing the truth.

I fight the way I heard my father from three rooms away.

With quick bites and punches in the gut.

Unforgivable and I can't hear why it matters.

I hate myself the way the dark voices taught me.

With a consuming passion and a destructive belief

that

                         I am not good enough.

If I close off my eyes with black lines like bird wings

you won't see any of this mind

that tried and tried to bleed through.

I want to be something horrible for the feeling of it.

My body feels big.

All that means is that I am sad

but it's easier to say than:

My childhood was broken into a thousand pieces

and I'm afraid it's too late to put them back together.

That means

I am broken.

That means

I'm afraid I will never know how to fix myself.

But I call it restless and

I call it tired.

Let's leave it at that tonight.

Pieces Pt. II:

I dyed my hair

but it doesn't mean anything.

I gave myself a piercing.

It stung.

Not enough.

I went to therapy.

It doesn't work if you don't want it to.

It doesn't work if you lie.

There was a year I was so obsessive

I worked out on Christmas morning.

and I didn't eat until a month after the new year.

An exercise addiction sounds ridiculous, sounds desirable.

Nothing takes the hurt away.

I don't know how to make you feel what it feels like to be

sixteen and unable to keep more than a bite down.

And still not thin.

Never, ever thin.

Someone told me yesterday that I was getting thick.

She meant it in a good way.

So why am I writing this now?

Everybody has emotional days.

Not everyone tallies them on their arms.

How the am I ever going to tell my daughter that she is

Somebody

if I still feel like

Nothing?

This Book:

If I write this and I let you read it

    Will you know me?

        Will you call me out?

But if I am recovered

there should be nothing to uncover.

There should be nothing dark to find.

They do not tell my story in the streets, in the churches

anymore.

        It's been too long for me to still be recovering.

12/22/2020

If I were a louder person I think I would spend

tonight at a bar performing spoken word and listening to

other poets cry out.

But poets who speak up

know how to break their hearts into bite sized pieces

and I serve mine whole or in silence.

I am truly a woman of my history.

We are full of words and love too big for our bodies to carry.

If I numbered these lines and

posted one at a time would

someone listen to what I'm saying?

A Picture of Myself as I am:

I am 18.

I spend a lot of time driving alone.

I feel like a stranger is living inside my body

They unzip me at night and sit with me until morning.

When I'm on the road I listen to music written by sad people.

They're people who feel like me except they know how to say it

without it coming out like a guilt trip or a cry for attention.

My father apologizes in mockery for being a failure.

He calls me one.

I don't spend much time writing anymore but I haven't found any new hobbies.

I am 18 and I am not sure of who loves me.

When there's silence I think about the people who used to and wish that I still knew them.

I remember that I'm glad I do not.

I'm 18 and I turn my face upwards.

The sky makes me feel small and I'm afraid of feeling like I am the center of any kind of universe.

Confidence is a dangerous fire.

I'm 18 and anorexia still knows my name.

I'll ask her to forget it time and time again but she comes

back and I don't tell her goodbye.

I'm 18 and

I'm still 18.

A Picture of Myself as I Wish I Were:

I would be the collage of art that makes a passersby stop

I would be a proud writer, musician, and friend.

I would have someone else to call.

I would remember to Love people.

I would remember to think in ways other than in color.

Not everyone thinks in color;

                    Black and white matters too.

I would be something more than nothing.

I would know how to write with a punch and a dollar sign

and leave these weeping lines behind.

I would know my mother behind her world weary mind,

she would know me behind my forgetful one.

I would be the only love he has known.

I would be healing, or

I would always have been whole.

I would not be angry.

I would not be sad.

I would not be jealous.

I would not be unkind.

A picture of myself as I am is a shaky frame askew.

A picture of myself as I wish I were is a picture of a picture of a picture of perfection.

It's Starting to Feel More Like Home:

Here,

with you,

in the sunlight,

on the old couch from your parent's house.

In the space separating me from the place I grew up,

there's peace.

Thinspiration:

I found you in my mother's eyes after a loud night.

I found you in my sister's shadow,

in her shadow,

in her shadow.

It isn't her fault she got the thinness and I got the eyes and
height of our heritage.

I don't look like a willowy Korean girl, just a mixed up one.

Just a lost one.

I'm sixteen miles away from home.

This place I am is a haven

still they reach out to me.

I need distance, please.

If I move into the mountains will you be able to see
me?

I find every way in the world to hide.

I talk about healing but I don't know what it feels like.

If I stay behind the camera will you know my name?

I talk about new places but I run in circles of teenage
dreams.

I didn't want to be the girl I was.

Regret keeps me inside her past.

This Valentine's day will be four years since the attempt.

I drove past the hospital a couple weeks ago.

It screamed my name,

it blinded me.

He asked me to come back to bed

and I didn't say,

> *I can't sit still,*

>> *even with you.*

>>> *I'm so tired of this girl.*
>>> *She needs changing,*
>>> *she needs changing,*
>>> *she needs to change.*

This was supposed to be an outpouring of old anorexic
feelings.

instead it has turned into a leaking of this old heart.

There's a Wrongness Somewhere:

I'm not quite home, but I don't feel alone anymore.
What's wrong with me?

Why would you want to spend the rest of your life filling all
these empty parts?
What's wrong with me?

I am not a whole person.
I've spent the last year and a half of my childhood trying to
outrun this sadness.
I only grew it bigger.
I cut holes in my skin so that I would be the one making the
holes.
I cut holes in my skin hoping they would be big enough to
swallow the real ones.
I'm flimsy and weak now.
I have nothing to me but the empty pieces.
You don't want to spend your whole life finding patches.
What's wrong with me?

When you are suicidal

and your best friends tells you it's too much and not

enough,

and a boy only a 16 year old could love

leaves every day for two years,

and your father won't look at you,

and your mother has five other people to look at,

you stay alone.

What's wrong with me?

I still think about you and her and the first time.

It still makes me sick.

By not telling me it's like you were still there, and I am

selfish and so full of needs

I need you all here.

I'm sorry I make everything about me,

you're just the first person to make me feel important.

It makes me so ugly and dependent.

It makes me hold on too tight

trying to make up for all the people who made me feel like

nothing.

I say that even though I am the one who has made me feel

the closest to nothing.

A Love Unending:

I want you with all the anger I have saved in my skin

and in poems and words I never said.

I want you with all the passion I didn't know how to express

when I was a smaller girl;

I want you with all the sadness I held inside my mind

until it leaked out and wrote a story;

That story was about a lonely girl until,

You.

I love you with all the frustration of not being understood

or known

and that being all that matters to your heart.

I love you with all the love I have ever received.

Love!

You!

You are the one I am giving it back to.

I love you with all the kindness I have felt,

and all of it that I had an opportunity to give and chose not

to.

I choose to now.

We know we need Love.

We learn how to wrap it up pretty and gift it

when there isn't time to make it nice.

We know how to hand it over without looking.

We know how to say I love you in a million different

tongues.

2/27/21

I hate that I am the same sad person in the kitchen of a new

home as I was in my teenage bedroom.

I'm not surprised.

I didn't expect everything to be perfect.

but I hate it.

I'm running and

running

and

running

always

running

from the next moment I realize

I have been deep places

and they haunt me.

4/8/21

I took a bath in sunshine and floated away.

When I landed I was in the place that used to be my brain.

It said,

>   *stay awhile.*

I said,

>   *Maybe I will.*

I walked past sinkholes and flashing exit signs,

I walked past a love of metaphors and the night sky,

past two boys with hidden hearts,

past an empty bed and a full garden.

I saw Loneliness and Isolation sitting side by side.

They did not see me.

They did not smile.

I was getting close to the shadows.

I knew what came next.

>   *Go ahead.*

>   *I don't want to. There's a stomach caving in*
>   *and a sink full of blood. I can see it.*
>   *I don't want to go back there.*

I opened my eyes and stared at the sun soaked wall.

I looked down at my body and all the wars it had fought.

I was glad to be on the other side of the river.

I was glad to be alive.

If I Were Writing:

If I were writing I would be a different woman.

If you are afraid you are going in the right direction,
fight through it.

We write because we need to, not because we want to.

If I were writing I would pray that I am always, always able
to hold on to the force that made me write a book and a half
before twenty.

If I were writing I would know I was doing that.

When I'm not writing, I'm not writing myself any
directions.

I'm in a fog of going nowhere,

Going somewhere is the closest I get to peace.

I have to go somewhere.

Stagnation is possibly my greatest fear,

a selfish one, but there it is.

If I sat still everything I wrote out of my blood would creep
back in.

There would be nowhere to run this time.

When you grow up at fourteen, you stay grown up.

When you are grown up you're supposed to handle things
like a grownup.

Adults don't cut.

Adults don't starve themselves.

Adults don't sit inside a glass house and wait for someone to
notice.

I'm not Friends With my body:

I say,

    love me better

to everyone

but the only word when I speak is

                            me.

I wonder if they were right to say I'm the most like our

father

I pray every night that it

                    isn't true.

Praying doesn't change my soul.

Self abuse doesn't change the genetics that make my body.

Like the woman who raised me

I know nothing in between.

If I turn the things that hurt me into poetry then I can say

it's only the art that hurts.

Then I can focus on the colors and I won't look at myself

anymore.

It makes me sad to look at myself.

I still think that if I can take control of the physical that the

mental will be easier.

I don't know another answer.

When I can't control the outside

the inside rages that I have failed again.

I still believe her.

How can I tell other girls they are perfect when all I see in

myself is the opposite?

Why can't I do better?

Maybe it's not my father, but my mother I am taking the

shape of.

Teenage Dreamer Goes to Work:

From the ages of 16 until 20 I work and work so that I can
have a dream,

so that I can be somebody.

I work until there's no blood left in my fingers and my brain
looks like an old woman's,

but I'm in love with how it feels to be moving.

I won't slow down.

I move early in the morning and I don't stop until the moon
is saying goodnight.

The sky changes colors with me, the important thing is that
we are changing.

The seasons and I are hand-in-hand,

we each have our moods.

We each know what burnout tastes like.

From 16 until 20 I write two books, I start a business, I fall
in love deeply and get married young.

From 16 until 20 I learn everything that I can and ask for
more.

From 16 until 20 I buy my first car, I move out of my
parents home, I build a new one.

From 16 until 20 there's a fire in my heart and I know that I have to share it or it will eat me alive.

From 16 until 20 I am a different being each morning.

From 16 until 20 I look for the girl inside every day and when I find her she looks a little bit older.

From 16 until 20 I feel like I am 35 or 40.

I feel old when I move, when I walk and other people can see it too.

They say I have grown up before my time and I agree with them, but

this is what I begged on my knees for.

From 16 until 20 I have bags resting under my eyes.

They look like the ones that I write about on other people.

From 16 until 20 I carry a bag of books with me.

It's all the ones I have written and not spoken about.

It's all the ones I have been too busy or tired to write.

From 16 until 20 I have my mother's profile but I carry my father's childish heart.

From 16 until 20 I never stop doing.

I plant a tree and I walk away from it.

From 16 until 20 I find a new face to look like every day and it still isn't enough.

From 16 to 20, I make up for the empty years of 13 to 16.

From 16 until 20 I outrun a place of peace and look for one to forget instead.

To be honest, this is 16 to 18.

I don't know what 19 and 20 will be for me yet.

I don't make art, I just put things together that sound okay.

I Look Through a Window and See Regret Sleeping:

Time is a keeper and I am his ward

I have my father's opportunist mindset,

my mother's constant feeling of inadequacy.

Time is a keeper and I am held captive.

There's never enough of you.

Once I see a place to move to I can't stop until I get there.

I'm running.

I'm outrunning my age.

I will never be 18 again.

I will never be a teenage dreamer again.

I moved too far too fast

Childhood is left behind me.

4/17/21

I don't know if it's from my parents, my lover, or it's in my
blood from a thousand generations ago,
but I have this unconquerable need to keep building,
moving, and trying.
And if I don't move then I am wasting time.
And if I don't move then I am wasting my youth.
And if I don't move then I am wasting away.
And if I don't move then
I AM NOT DOING ENOUGH.
I am not doing enough
I am not doing enough.
I   am   not   doing   enough.
It is such a defeating and discouraging thing to give and give
and give
and for your own mind to still

                ask

                    for

                        more.

When the Girl Inside Gets Sad:

There are mornings when I wake up and know it will be
hard to find the bright spots.
There are days I walk through without seeing a thing.
On my lunch break, I sat in my car and I couldn't breathe.

> I felt so heavy.

And the blood came back.

> The fear.

I want to be a big sister, a new story.
I know that's what's wanted of me.

> *You've had so much life for eighteen.*

I hate it every single day.
I know I sound older than I am,

> and I can't find a carefree nature in the length

> of my clothes or the smile on my face.

I know it looks like I'm trying to fast forward, like I'm going
too fast.
That's all I know.
If I was a child it was selfish.

> If I dressed my age it was slutty.

There's a line to cross when you grow up.

I don't know if I ran or was pushed across it.

I just know I can't go back.

What the Remnants of an Unanswered ED Look Like:

I will be 19 years old in a week.

I will be married in 3.

I'm following a pattern, I'm following each day.

Teenage dreamer.

Teenage love.

Teenage talent.

Teenage sadness.

Teenage joy.

Grow out of it, my Love.

>You are none of those things and nothing else.

My body hurts with everything it has gone through.

My hands hurt from all the punishment they have dealt.

When she says,

>*She's even smaller than that other girl.*

When she says,

>*She's so tiny. She could fall apart.*

My dearest Ana turns to me with accusation that

>I am not that girl.

>(that I am still not that tiny girl.)

Have I not hurt enough to have the thinness I want?

Have I not sweat enough yet to empty myself of every piece too big?

That girl.

She and I starved next to each other at 14.

Her and I shared the same knife, the same scars, the same strict roof over our heads.

She was the first one who said,

> *I haven't eaten in a month.*

It made me run my own 28 days of empty plates,

empty hands, empty bellies.

Until my mother threatened,

> *It is recovery forced or recovery*
> *chosen, but it has to be one.*

You don't know her like I do.

I know where her demons live.

I know the white lines they sit in.

For the first time in my life I feel like I fit in with the size smalls.

It still isn't enough.

I have been hungry for 5 years.

As a teenager, I have dreamt of the end.

On 19:

It's 19 and one more year of teenage dreaming.

It's another day of cloudy joy,

another year of rich rain.

I promise you,

I am not done living.

I am not done dreaming.

Everyone has heard of the restlessness,

I haven't spoken much about learning to be still.

19 is past the 4 a.m. poetry and asking,

Who will I be tomorrow?

I know by now that tomorrow is always someone new.

There are worse things to be than changing.

19 is work and working towards the castle in the clouds.

19 is promising a never ending love.

It is knowing how to receive it too.

19 is an expedition into the woods.

It is knowing when it's time to come home.

19 is

one more day,

one more week,

one more year

I can say,

> *I'm happy to be here*

and mean it.

6/22/21

If we are in love we are the sun and the sun is a planet

spinning around us.

6/29/21

I have a burning anger towards wasted time.

Maybe it is because my mother has spent 25 years married to

a man she is not in love with

or because my father thinks he is a big man but he is nothing

but a loud voice.

I am going to make this life into something.

I am going to be somebody.

I am going to have my own voice and I do not have to tether

it any longer.

I've known the regret of missing time since I was 6 years old

and I never ever want to feel that way again.

Should I Disappear You Must Promise to Keep Loving People:

Don't you worry, Love, should I disappear.

I've only gone as far as the ocean;

I needed a little salt to balance out the sweetness of us.

/

Don't you worry, Mother,

if I don't come home this week.

I've only gone as far as the moon;

I was looking for a place where I could sit in the hollowness

and shine comfortably.

/

Don't you worry, Sister,

if I haven't called.

I've only gone into the silence of a wolf on the hunt for her

next meal;

The wild wanted me to come home and I could not resist.

/

Don't you worry, Poetry,

if I haven't visited you.

I've only gone as far as my next tempest.

We know they come often and unexpectedly.

I will always find you again.

/

Just wait for Autumn,

just wait for the wind,

just wait for the love,

just wait for the patience,

just wait for tension to walk away,

just wait for the peace.

/

Someday I will have a glorious return to the light.

It is worth waiting for.

We Will be Home:

I've been living in some day dreams,

I've been trying to make it by.

There are so many pieces of sunshine I don't write about

anymore,

there are so many moonless nights I am not

struck with poetry.

I don't know if it's aging, or simply a different age

but I'm not the girl I was.

Dreams look a little more hazy, a little more like tomorrow

and next year, instead of "in a forest somewhere".

I'm home building.

I'm love growing.

I'm working to be the woman who I see in my future.

I do still write about it.

In smaller pieces, in the spaces there is time.

You'll hear from me.

Please write back.

A Little Bit Sleepy, a Little Bit Better:

In the fullness of love I am resting.

There is a good man who holds me and a warm home.

Most days I am eating, half of the days my mind is dry.

Still, I want to be well to the absolute.

Maybe I will go and talk to someone who knows.

Maybe I will go and talk to God.

I want to be whole.

One More Small Musing:

Through the wear and tear I've fought through

I'm feeling dreamy.

You would think the rosy colors would have faded more

after this life I've lived.

Maybe I would be a better writer if I wrote about someone

else.

Someone other than me.

But if I've learned anything so far

it's this girl inside I live with.

I know my hills and valleys like a winter knows snow,

like a garden grows,

like a river moves.

It's the hurting that changed me.

Nothing changes it back and I have to stop trying.

Regret is such a joyless word.

If I weren't alive I would never have known him

I would never have been in love.

You Say Natural is Best, I Say Living is:

I know that things like

giving myself a piercing,

getting my first tattoo,

changing my hair

can seem so vain and surface level.

I know that they probably are.

To me and my art gallery brain, they mean something.

If nothing else they mean I am on my way somewhere.

Like I am on my way to being the girl I dream of being.

They say,

> *This is me.*
>
> *I have lived,*
>
> *I have fought wars,*
>
> *I have survived*
>
> *and I'm here to tell the story.*

They say,

> *I have loved*
>
> *I have been loved*
>
> *I have given everything*
>
> *and I have been given so much in return.*

I know that it is going to take digging deeper into my soul

than I would care to know is possible

for the remains of what started out as a childhood

to take the shape of anything like a good home.

Honestly, I don't feel ready to break up

how this outside face is masking the hidden tangles yet.

It's scary to look back at the things that changed you.

But the brown rug of my living room is starting to take the

size of an elephant and

I think everyone I invite in is whispering about it behind my

back.

Hearing them and still saying,

I am okay.

It's not time yet.

But I want to

Be still.

I want to remember how good it feels

When Love Begins.

I want to carry my sisters with me as deep as the blood in my

veins.

We are a garden.

I want, more than anything, to live, to love, and to grow.

I need change.

But I need it for the Girl Inside.

I pray to God that all the hurting, desperate, grey and blue,

cloudy, lonely, restless, fearful, moving, artful, anxious,

injured, scraped, bruised, healing, planting, nostalgic,

throbbing, building, sweet, sad

ones like her

will find the peace and understanding that they most long

for.

I pray to God,

someday I will find rest with them too.

July:

I am afraid people I know are going to read this and say I am Godless.

I am not.

I am just being honest for this one book.

I am just hurting.

7/16/21

I understand that I am small.

That's not where the restlessness comes from.

I feel sick,

I feel lost,

I feel stuck.

It's not his fault.

It's not because of him.

My childhood still holds me so tight.

Let me go.

I cannot have a small life.

I cannot have a still life.

Let me move.

For Him:

The world stops spinning once more out of a million times.

    "They found a mass in my chest."

No.

    No,   no,   no,   no,   no,   no.

    The world stops spinning one more time.

    "They think it's cancer."

But you are so good.

You are so young.

But I grew up with you.

I don't know what to give you.

I only have crying thoughts, crying words.

I don't have anything. I don't have any control.

Take my stupid caring, little as it is.

I am so small next to everyone else who loves you, but I'm here.

I'll always be here.

    The world stops spinning one more time.

I remember every moment of a memory.

This is the poison we pray against.

The world stops spinning one more time.

I can hear everyone's sadness, but I hear the singing and praises too.

God knows this valley.

Slowly,   slowly,   slowly

We will start spinning again

It's Wednesday:

How many times can I say I am

                              restless

        before something changes?

It has to be so old to hear.

I know my ears, my hands drag from how many times I have

written and spoken that word.

My Love tells me putting ink in my skin will not fill me up,

will not replace the soul deep sting I am missing.

My Love tells me putting another needle through my ear is

not what I need to feel like a person I could love.

He is right in most worlds, I think, but not I think,

in mine.

If I look like the girl I want to be, will it change me into her?

If I write like I am something big and glamorous,

you can't see me through this page.

It's just me, after all of it.

It's just the shadow of me.

Impatience or My Driving Force:

Life is short and I have been painfully aware of that for as long as I can remember.

Since my grandfather passed away when I was six years old and I first felt the regret of

> *I didn't try hard enough.*
>
> *I didn't know him well enough.*

That was the first time I decided for myself I did not deserve to live.

I knew he had loved me oh so deeply.

I knew I had not loved him back as well.

I promised myself I would try my best to never feel that way again.

But cancer is cancer, and it will come again.

I next met it with my teenage best friend.

Again I felt,

> *I haven't reached out enough.*
>
> *I haven't called enough.*
>
> *I have not loved well enough.*

Regret, may be a worse enemy to me than stillness.

You know my heart, you know my restless heart.

You know how much this means to me.

I never want to feel like I have wasted time.

   I never want to feel like I have wasted love.

      I never want to feel like I have wasted my

life.

         I don't want to wait for twenty.

         I don't want to wait for tomorrow.

         I don't want to wait for next week.

         I live now. I love now.

Sitting in a Square of Natural light:

I may not have peace,

I may not have rest,

but I have love.

For the Girl Inside and Ones Like Her:

We have been the hurricane and we have walked out alive.

We have seen a lightless life and we decide we want more.

/

When you wake up into those mornings where *upbeat message*

you know you loved or in love,

you can feel the sun on your skin,

you move your body and it feels right,

you nourish yourself and it feels welcome,

hold onto those.

This is why we fought to stay alive.

These are the days we live for.

If I am Going to Speak it Will be With Honesty:

I'm 19 and I feel like I'm carrying the

whole world in my arms.

This is me promising that I will never let my children drag

my past the way I am laden down with my parents.

My mother doesn't speak of it often,

but I know that the hurt of Highschool has not left her

hallways.

I know her own poetry days are still digging underneath her

skin.

My father speaks of Michigan with a false pride.

He can't admit that he did not have a kind father and he let

it turn him into

     the same anger,

          the same shout-you-down voice,

               the same kind of egotistical man.

He won't speak to me if he reads this,

like he could not look me in the eyes after *When Love*

Begins.

Like he chose not to speak to me for half a year after calling

me

an attention seeker,

a screw up,

after saying I never tried to love

him.

He doesn't understand the sacrifice of letting go of every

storm I ever listened to.

Those are the lessons I have from him.

How to destroy a marriage.

How to tear down a home.

I never want to be that.

Unable to change what I do not like about myself.

I want control.

I want power over myself.

God, let me never allow my pride to matter more than

people.

I Wrote About You:

I wrote about putting down the knife.

I wrote about living through nights like that to write like
this.

I wrote about how my mother deserves the daughter I could
never be,

I wrote about how my father has been more thunder and
rain than father.

I wrote about how much love I have felt missing, and how
much I have given out, and how much I have received.

I wrote about how I wear the mask everyone in recovery
wears.

I wrote about how my sisters and brothers are stronger in
different ways than me,

but I am still so terrified they will see my scars and follow my
shadow.

I wrote about how the thought of motherhood petrifies me.

I wrote about how loneliness sticks.

I wrote about beautiful things and snowy trees.

I wrote about searching.

I wrote about the Love of my life.

I wrote about all the hurt, all the hunger, all the trying to

heal.

I don't know what's next.

If I am restless for a place I have never been to,

how do I find out where that is?

I thought poetry was the path to home,

but it's turning into another dead end road.

Walking in circles and walking in circles and walking.

Where is the girl inside today?

Thank You:

After 122 pages of mood swings thank you if you are
still walking beside me.
After so many goodbyes and
so many departures without goodbyes,
I will do my best to never take for granted the people who
stay.

E.G. or Eden Gayle is a photographer and writer from Columbus, Ohio.

For the Girl Inside and Ones Like Her is her second poetry collection, following after her debut book, *When Love Begins.*

Eden plans to continue writing, creating, learning, and exploring nature.

When not immersed in her creative work, Eden loves to hike with her husband, play violin, and travel.

You can follow her adventures at:

Instagram: @edengayle31 or @_e.g._photos
Facebook: @edengayle31

Made in the USA
Monee, IL
19 October 2021

80390258R10080